GOLDEN SCORES

AVORITE FILM SELECTIONS ARRANGED ... VEREN

— PIANO LEVEL —
LATE INTERMEDIATE

ISBN 978-1-4950-9438-5

HAL•LEONARD®

7777 W. BLUEMOUND RD. P.O. BOX 13819 MILWAUKEE, WI 53213

Visit Hal Leonard Online at
www.halleonard.com

Visit Phillip at
www.phillipkeveren.com

PREFACE

Golden Scores is the first folio that establishes a new category, Piano Solo Plus, in *The Phillip Keveren Series*. In addition to single title piano solos, you will find medleys – in this case, one medley from a film composer (John Barry) and one medley from a film (*The Wizard of Oz*) – and two vocal/piano arrangements, "Moon River" and "Over the Rainbow."

Music written specifically for the cinema has become an integral fixture in the music of our time. It is not uncommon to hear the best of this genre included in symphony orchestra programs, and many of the finest "serious" composers of the 20th and 21st centuries (Aaron Copland, John Corigliano, et al.) have written film scores.

I hope this Piano Solo Plus collection will be a welcome addition to your music library.

Sincerely,

Phillip Keveren

BIOGRAPHY

Phillip Keveren, a multi-talented keyboard artist and composer, has composed original works in a variety of genres from piano solo to symphonic orchestra. Mr. Keveren gives frequent concerts and workshops for teachers and their students in the United States, Canada, Europe, and Asia. Mr. Keveren holds a B.M. in composition from California State University Northridge and a M.M. in composition from the University of Southern California.

CONTENTS

AS TIME GOES BY
from CASABLANCA

Words and Music by
HERMAN HUPFELD
Arranged by Phillip Keveren

Rubato (♩ = c. 88)

Steady Jazz Ballad (♩ = 76)

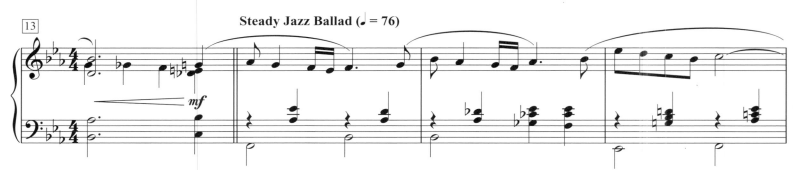

JOHN BARRY MEDLEY

Arranged by Phillip Keveren

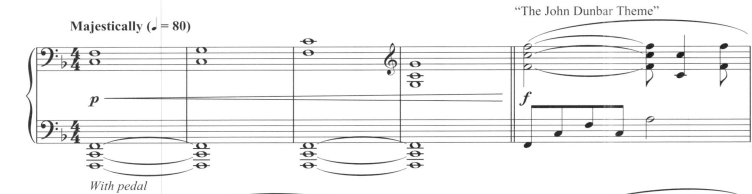

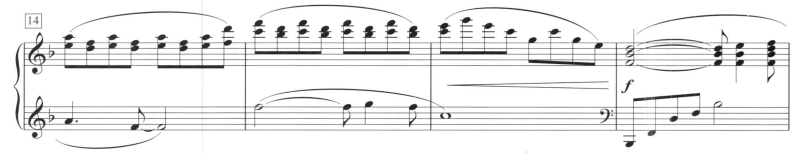

THE JOHN DUNBAR THEME
from DANCES WITH WOLVES
By JOHN BARRY

"The Music of Goodbye"

THE MUSIC OF GOODBYE
from OUT OF AFRICA
Words and Music by JOHN BARRY, ALAN BERGMAN and MARILYN BERGMAN

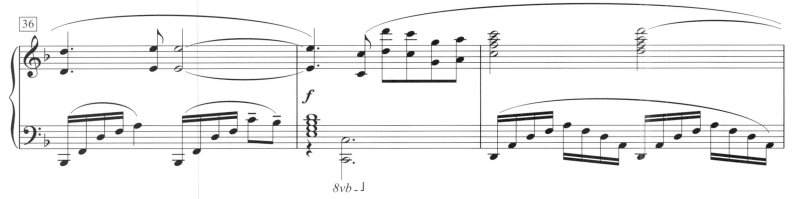

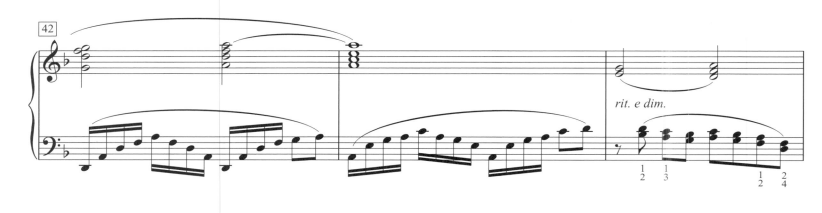

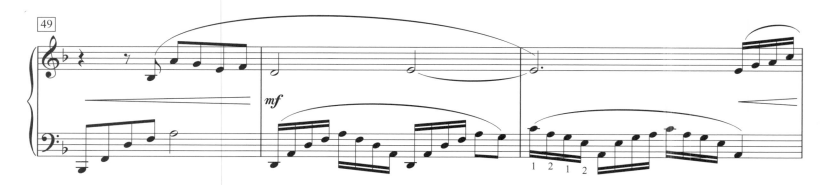

9

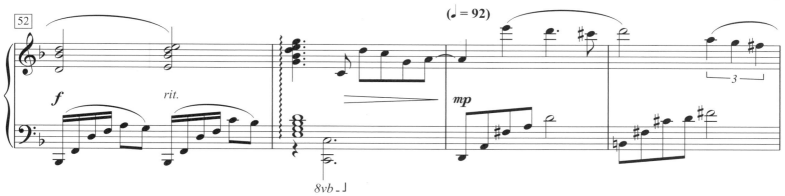

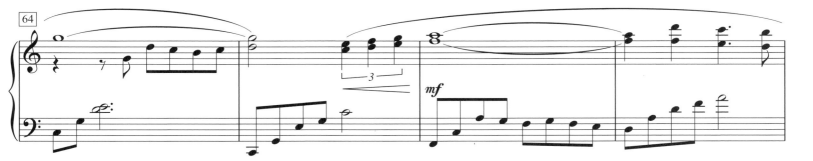

SOMEWHERE IN TIME
from SOMEWHERE IN TIME
By JOHN BARRY
Copyright © 1980 USI B GLOBAL MUSIC PUBLISHING
This arrangement Copyright © 2018 USI B GLOBAL MUSIC PUBLISHING
All Rights Controlled and Administered by SONGS OF UNIVERSAL, INC.
All Rights Reserved   Used by Permission

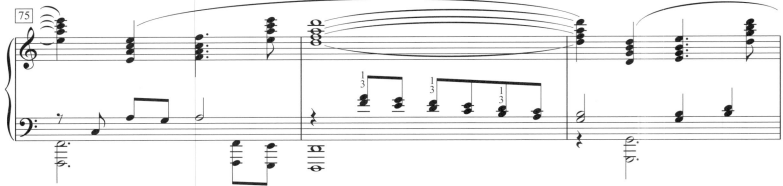

"We Have All the Time in the World"

Lyrically (♩ = 100)

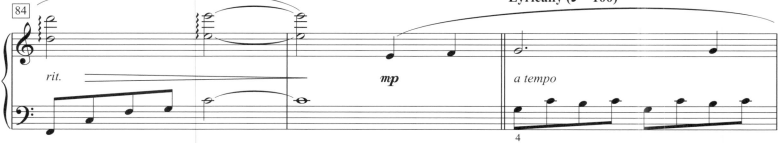

WE HAVE ALL THE TIME IN THE WORLD
from ON HER MAJESTY'S SECRET SERVICE
Music by JOHN BARRY
Lyrics by HAL DAVID

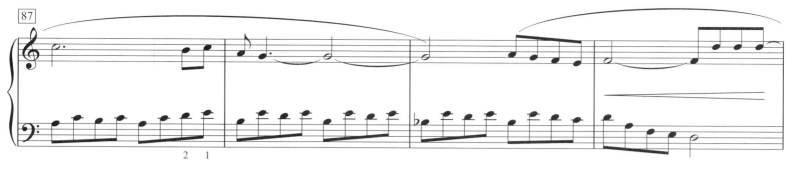

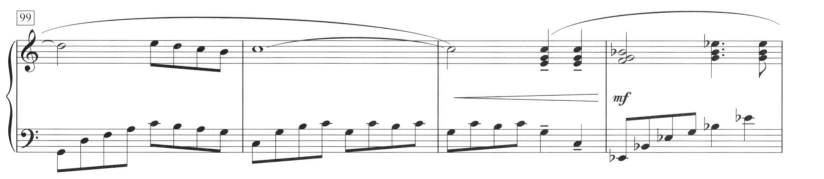

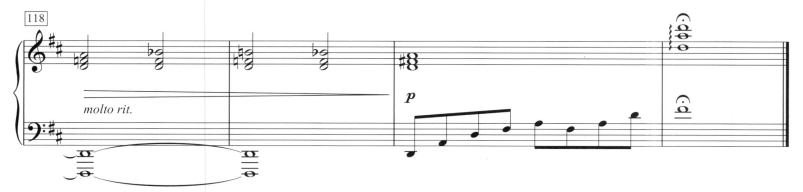

THE GODFATHER WALTZ

from the Paramount Pictures THE GODFATHER, GODFATHER II, and GODFATHER III

By NINO ROTA
Arranged by Phillip Keveren

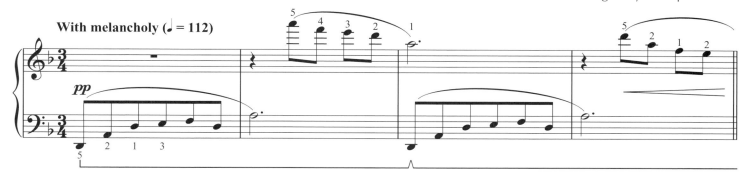

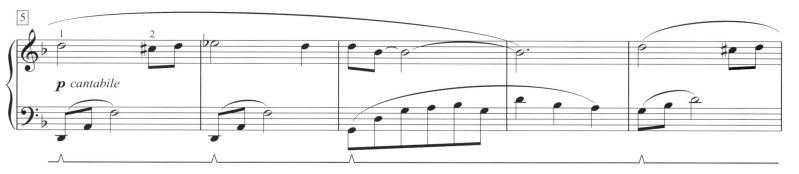

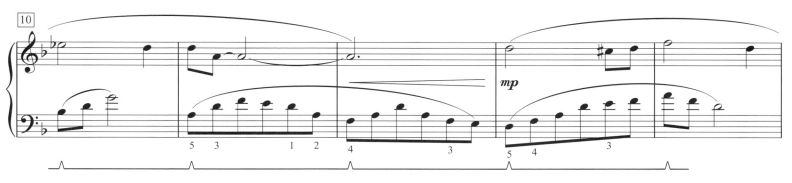

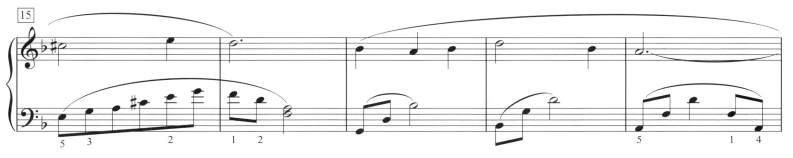

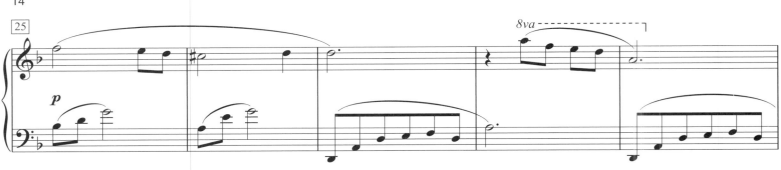

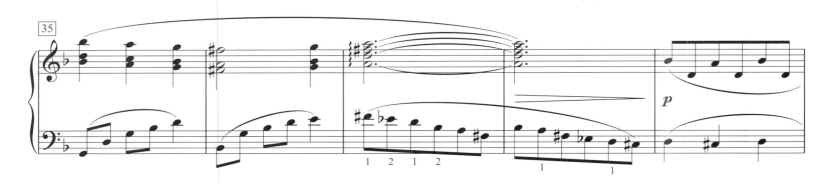

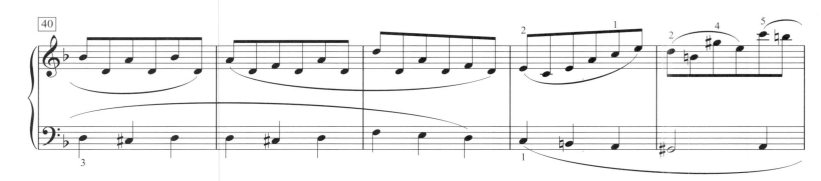

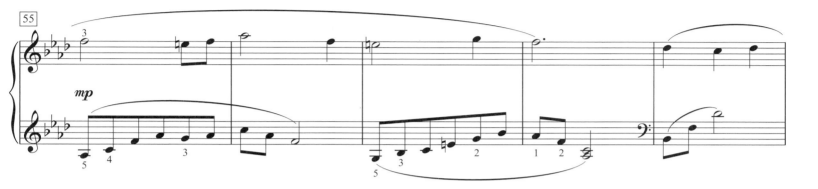

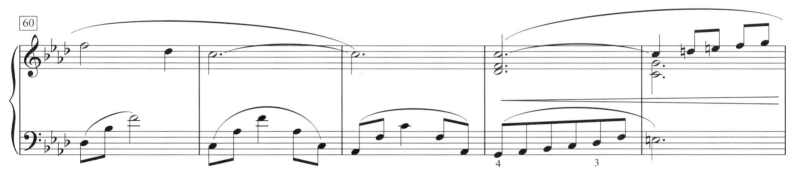

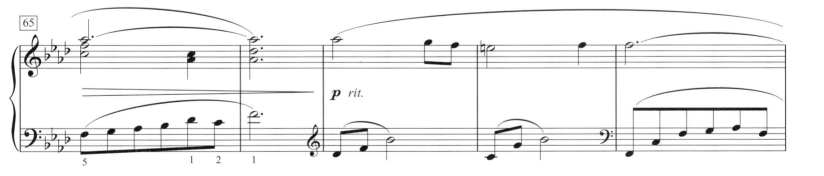

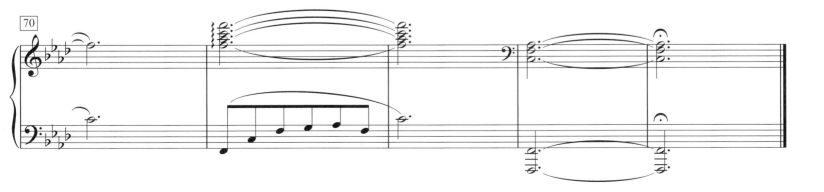

DON'T RAIN ON MY PARADE

from FUNNY GIRL

Words by BOB MERRILL
Music by JULE STYNE
Arranged by Phillip Keveren

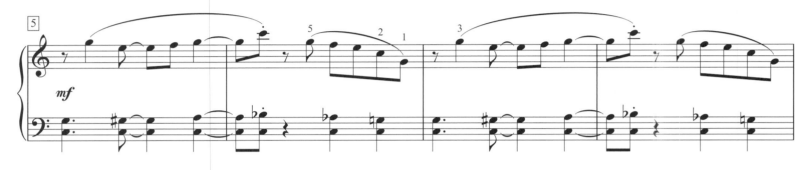

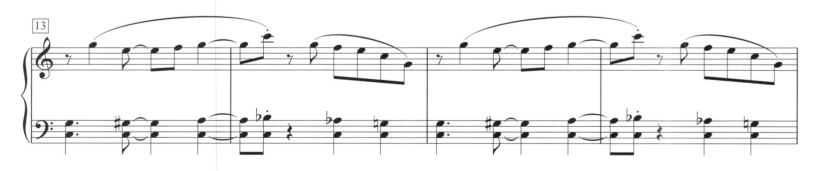

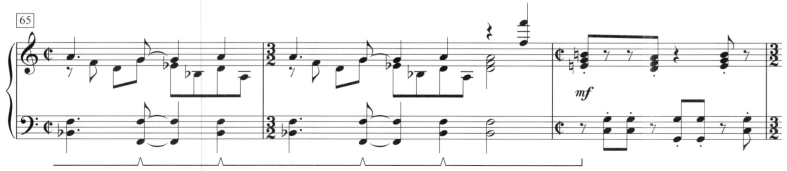

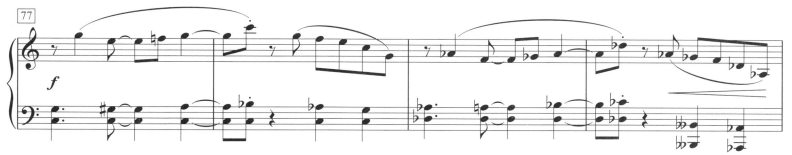

MOON RIVER

from the Paramount Picture BREAKFAST AT TIFFANY'S

Words by JOHNNY MERCER
Music by HENRY MANCINI
Arranged by Phillip Keveren

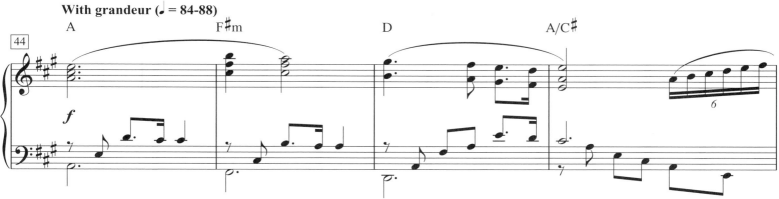

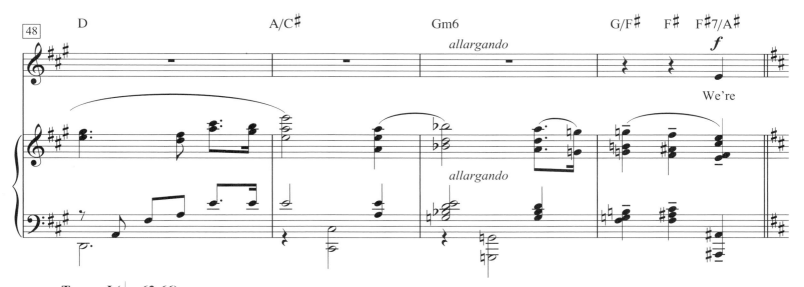

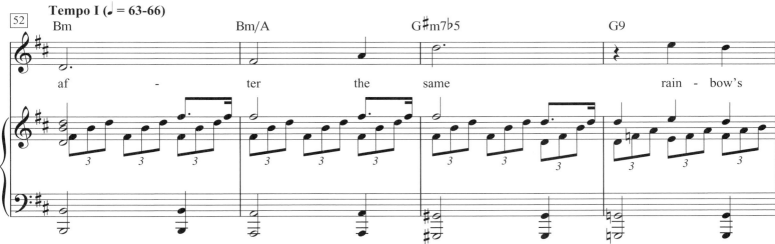

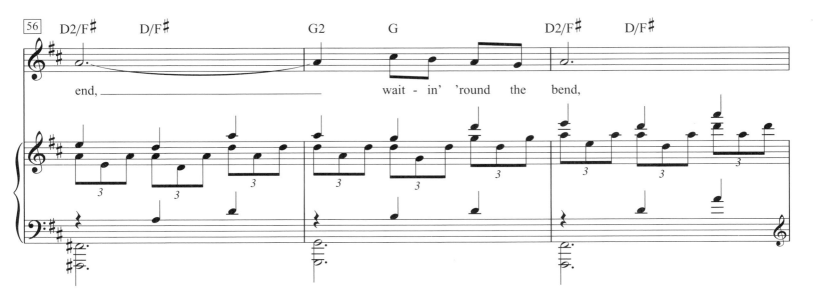

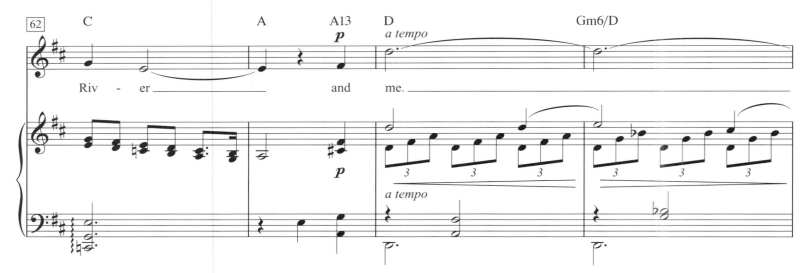

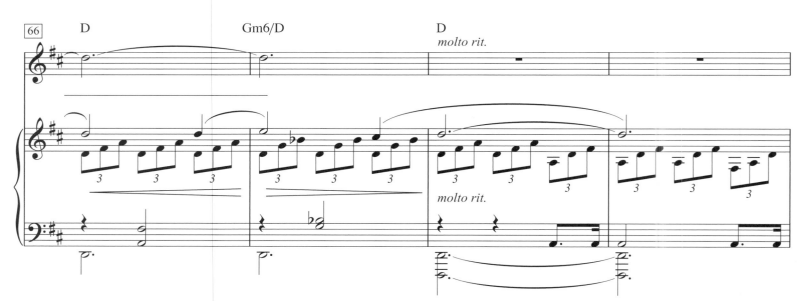

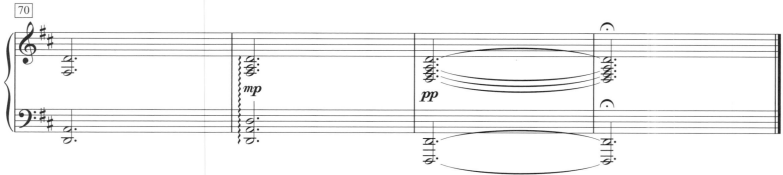

MY HEART WILL GO ON
(Love Theme From 'Titanic')
from the Paramount and Twentieth Century Fox Motion Picture TITANIC

Music by JAMES HORNER
Lyric by WILL JENNINGS
Arranged by Phillip Keveren

Atmospheric, rubato (♩ = c. 80)

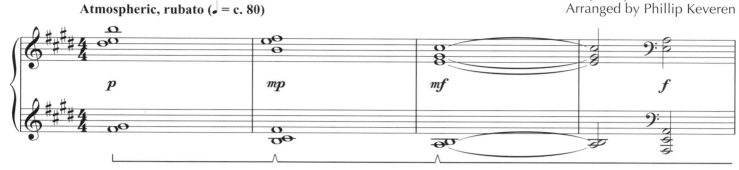

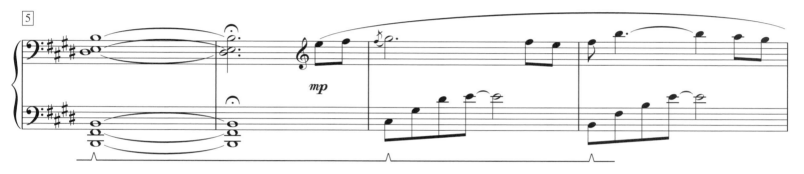

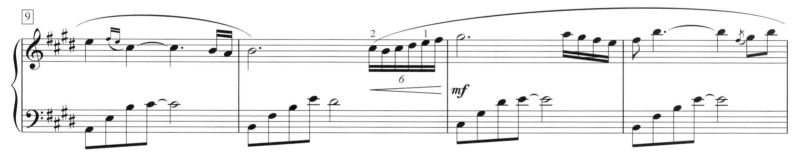

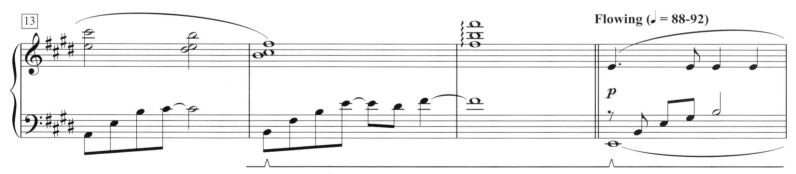

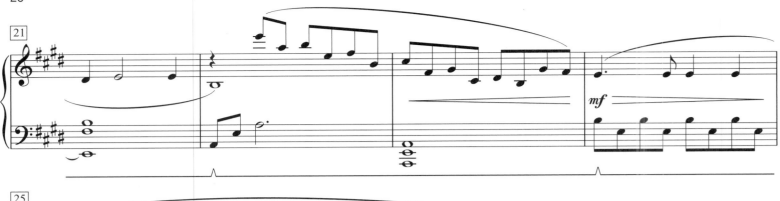

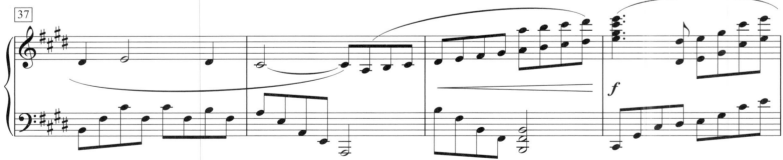

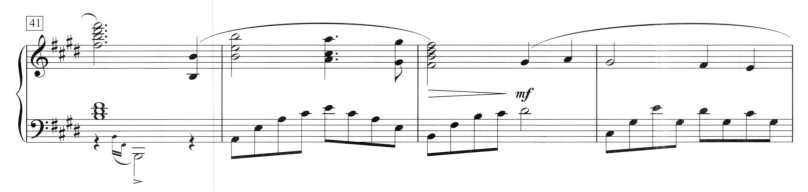

Slower, yet more passionately (♩ = 72-76)

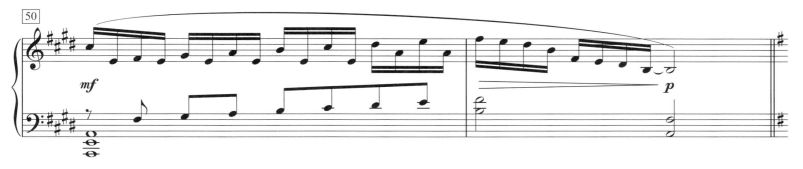

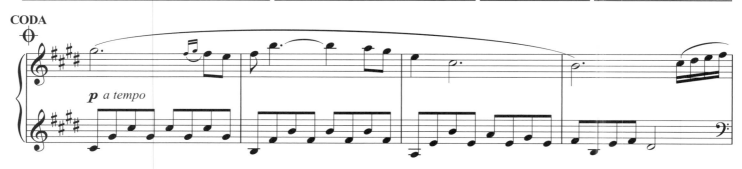

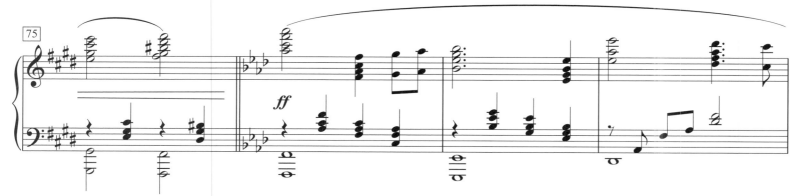

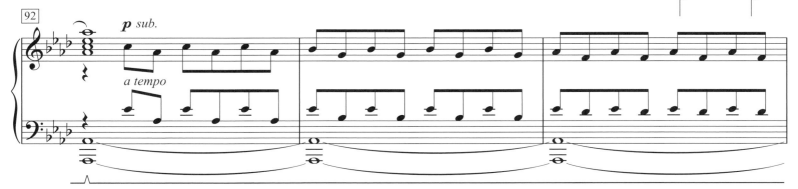

OVER THE RAINBOW
from THE WIZARD OF OZ

Music by HAROLD ARLEN
Lyric by E.Y. "YIP" HARBURG
Arranged by Phillip Keveren

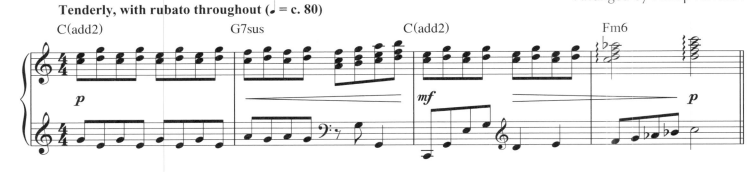

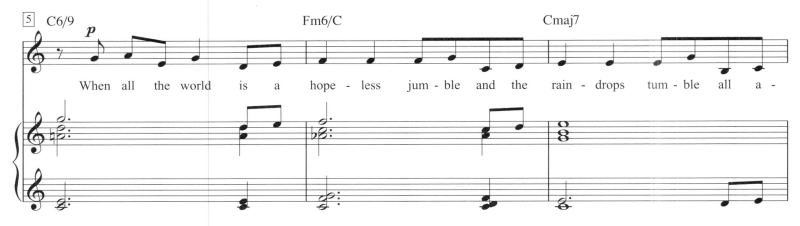

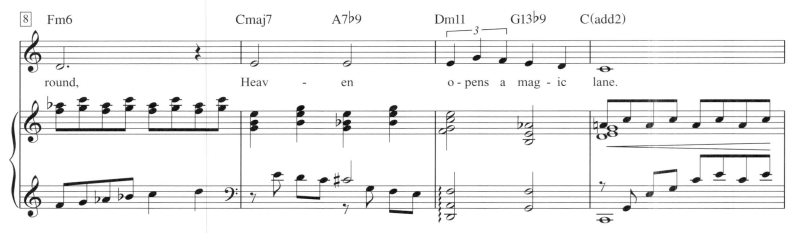

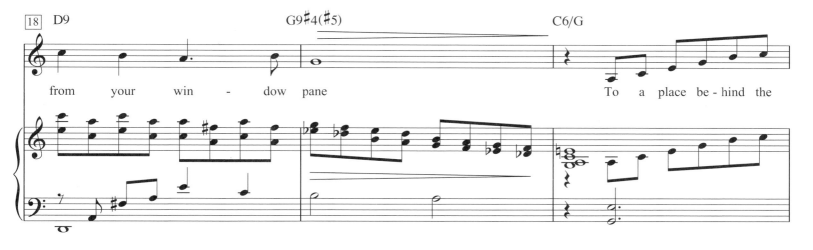

day I'll wish up-on a star and wake up where the clouds are far be-hind me. _____

_____ Where trou-bles melt like lem-on drops, a way, a-bove the chim-ney tops, that's

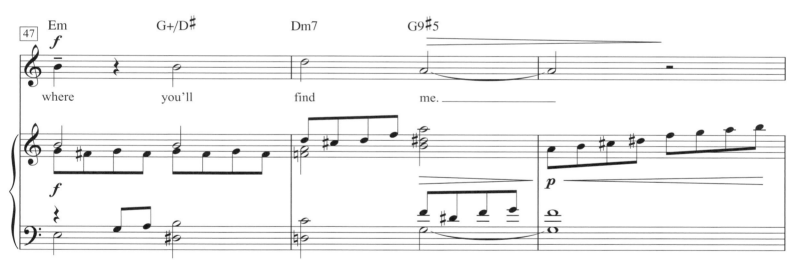

where you'll find me. _____

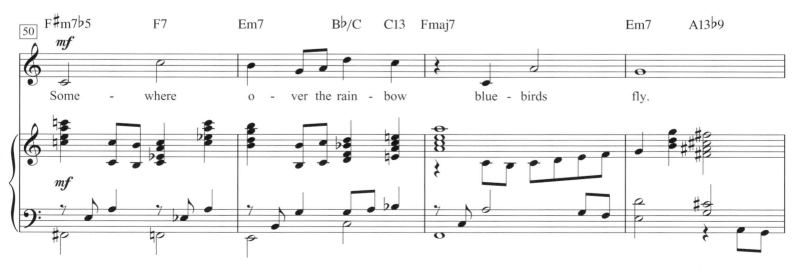

Some - where o - ver the rain - bow blue-birds fly.

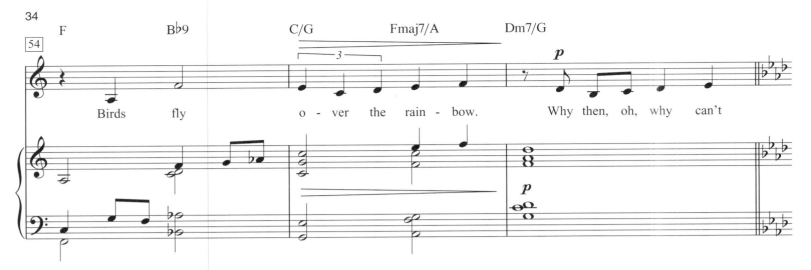

F B♭9 C/G Fmaj7/A Dm7/G

Birds fly o - ver the rain - bow. Why then, oh, why can't

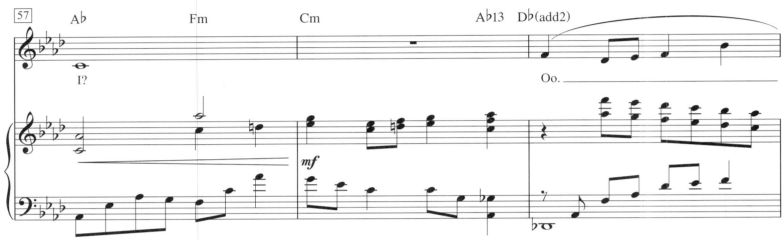

A♭ Fm Cm A♭13 D♭(add2)

I? Oo. _____

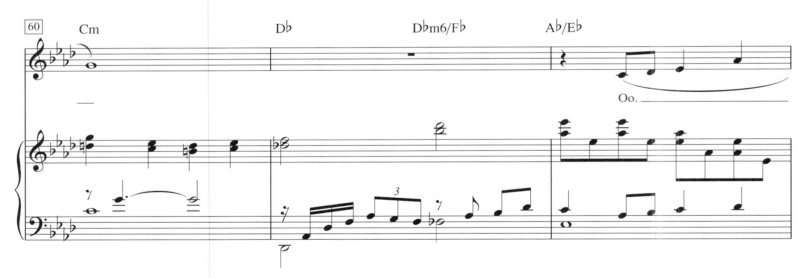

Cm D♭ D♭m6/F♭ A♭/E♭

Oo. _____

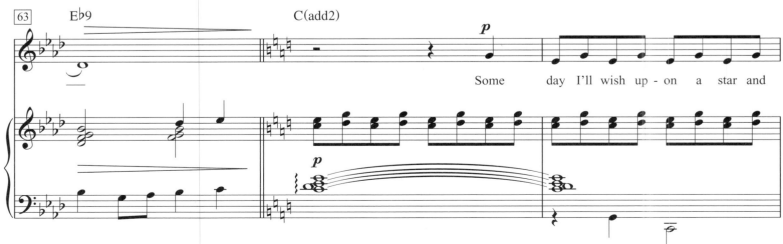

E♭9 C(add2)

Some day I'll wish up - on a star and

THAT'S ENTERTAINMENT
from THE BAND WAGON

Words by HOWARD DIETZ
Music by ARTHUR SCHWARTZ
Arranged by Phillip Keveren

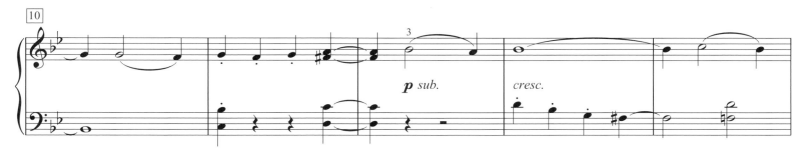

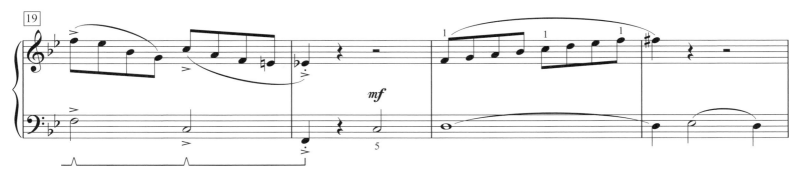

SINGIN' IN THE RAIN

from SINGIN' IN THE RAIN

Lyric by ARTHUR FREED
Music by NACIO HERB BROWN
Arranged by Phillip Keveren

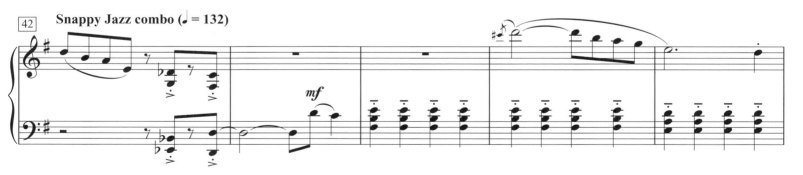

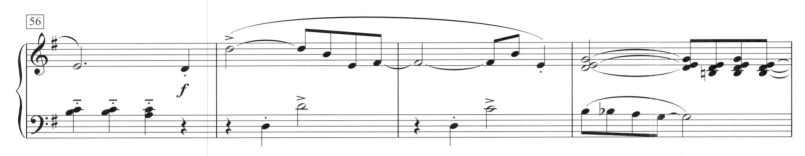

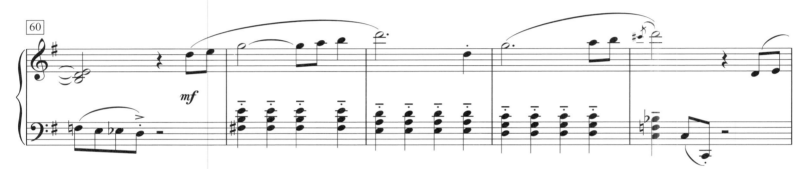

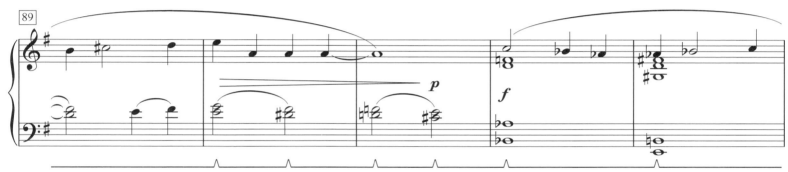

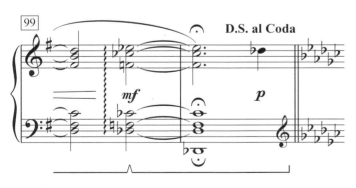

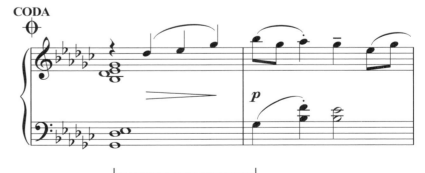

THE WIZARD OF OZ MEDLEY

Lyric by E.Y. "YIP" HARBURG
Music by HAROLD ARLEN
Arranged by Phillip Keveren

Fanfare (♩ = 100)

With pedal

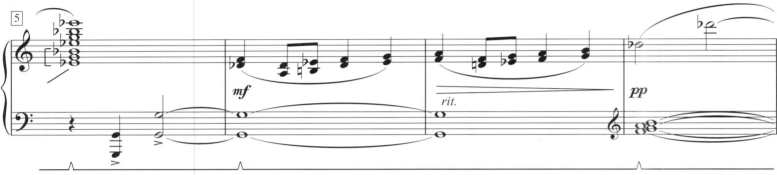

"Ding-Dong! The Witch Is Dead"
Brightly (♩ = 108)

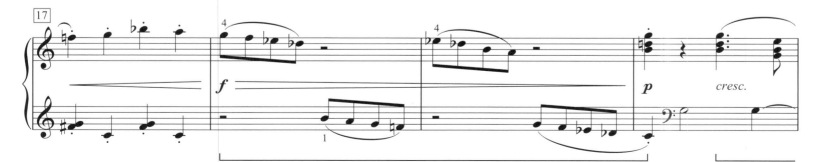

"If I Only Had a Brain"

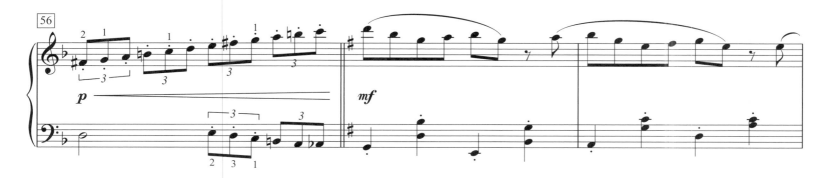

"Lullaby League and Lollipop Guild"

Sprightly (♩ = 144) (♪♪ = ♪♪)

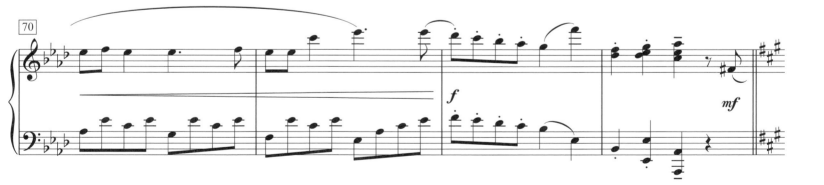

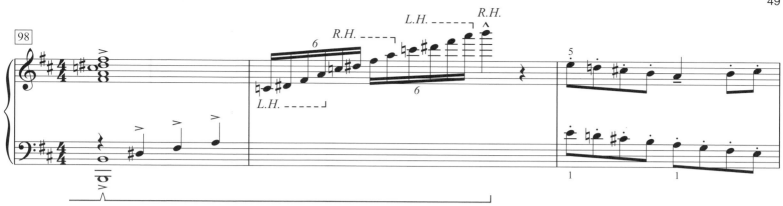

Tenderly, with rubato throughout (♩ = c. 80)

"Over the Rainbow"

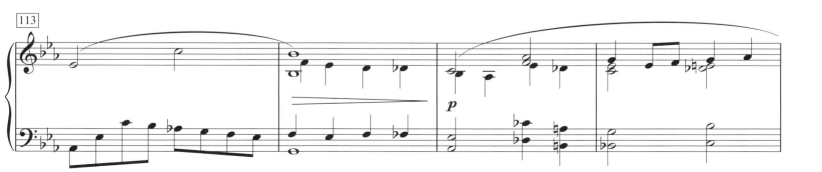

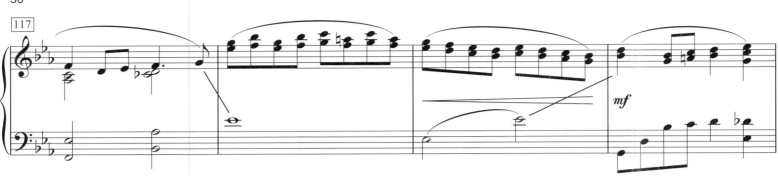

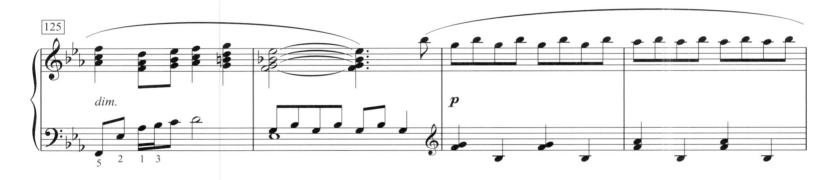

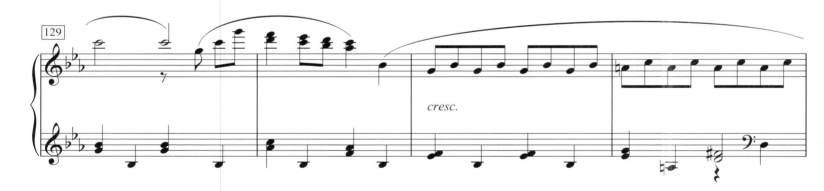

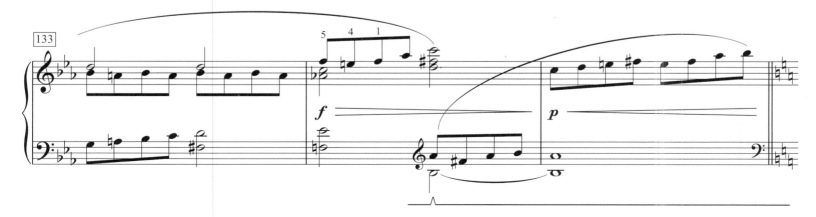

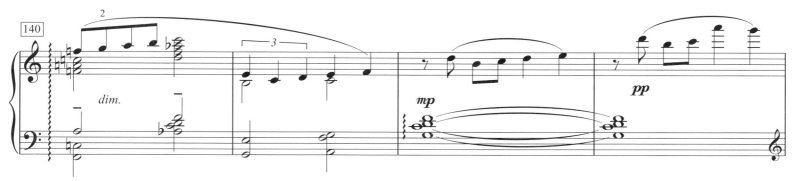

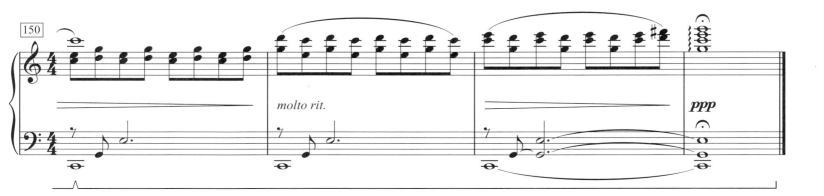

TO KILL A MOCKINGBIRD
(Main Title)
from TO KILL A MOCKINGBIRD

By ELMER BERNSTEIN
Arranged by Phillip Keveren

Poignantly, with rubato (♩ = c. 96-100)

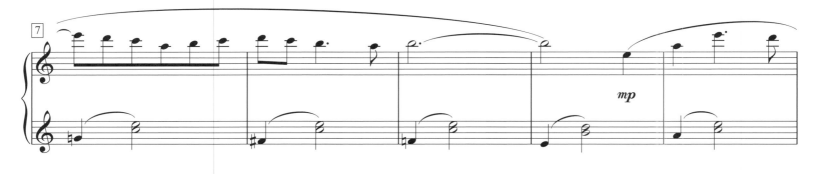

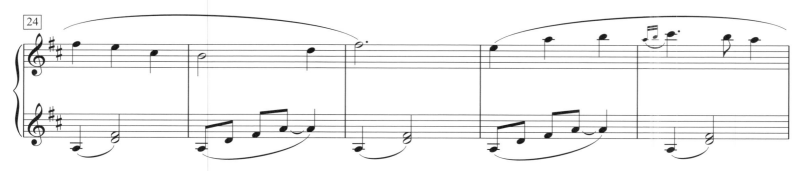

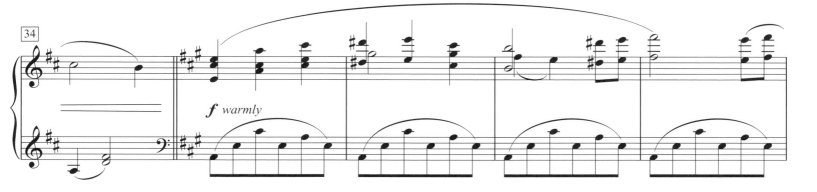

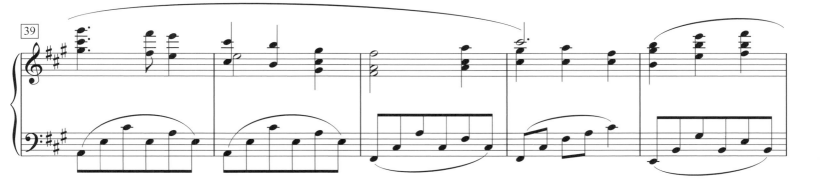

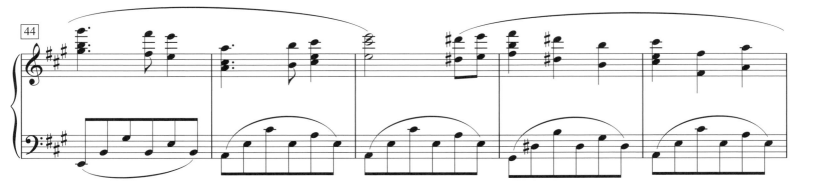

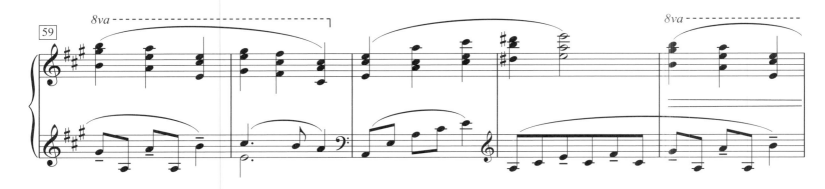

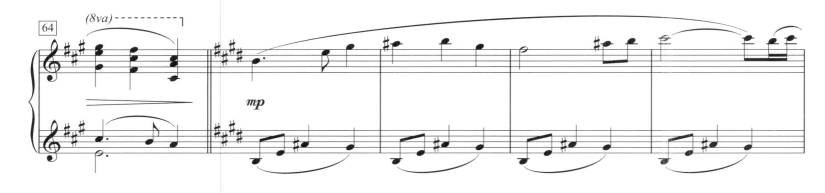

THE PHILLIP KEVEREN SERIES

PIANO SOLO

ABBA FOR CLASSICAL PIANO
00156644...$14.99

ABOVE ALL
00311024...$11.95

AMERICANA
00311348...$10.95

BACH MEETS JAZZ
00198473...$14.99

THE BEATLES
00306412...$16.99

THE BEATLES FOR CLASSICAL PIANO
00312189...$14.99

BEST PIANO SOLOS
00312546...$14.99

BLESSINGS
00156601...$12.99

BLUES CLASSICS
00198656...$12.99

BROADWAY'S BEST
00310669...$14.99

A CELTIC CHRISTMAS
00310629...$12.99

THE CELTIC COLLECTION
00310549...$12.95

CHRISTMAS PRAISE HYMNS
00236669...$12.99

CHRISTMAS MEDLEYS
00311414...$12.99

CHRISTMAS AT THE MOVIES
00312190...$14.99

CHRISTMAS SONGS FOR CLASSICAL PIANO
00233788...$12.99

CHRISTMAS WORSHIP MEDLEYS
00311769...$12.99

CINEMA CLASSICS
00310607...$14.99

CLASSIC WEDDING SONGS
00311101...$10.95

CLASSICAL JAZZ
00311083...$12.95

COLDPLAY FOR CLASSICAL PIANO
00137779...$14.99

CONTEMPORARY WEDDING SONGS
00311103...$12.99

DISNEY SONGS FOR CLASSICAL PIANO
00311754...$16.99

FIDDLIN' AT THE PIANO
00315974...$12.99

THE FILM SCORE COLLECTION
00311811...$14.99

GOSPEL GREATS
00144351...$12.99

THE GREAT AMERICAN SONGBOOK
00183566...$12.99

THE GREAT MELODIES
00312084...$12.99

GREAT STANDARDS
00311157...$12.95

THE HYMN COLLECTION
00311071...$12.99

HYMN MEDLEYS
00311349...$12.99

HYMNS WITH A TOUCH OF JAZZ
00311249...$12.99

I COULD SING OF YOUR LOVE FOREVER
00310905...$12.95

JINGLE JAZZ
00310762...$14.99

BILLY JOEL FOR CLASSICAL PIANO
00175310...$14.99

ELTON JOHN FOR CLASSICAL PIANO
00126449...$14.99

LET FREEDOM RING!
00310839...$9.95

ANDREW LLOYD WEBBER
00313227...$15.99

MANCINI MAGIC
00313523...$12.99

MORE DISNEY SONGS FOR CLASSICAL PIANO
00312113...$15.99

THE MOST BEAUTIFUL SONGS FOR EASY CLASSICAL PIANO
00233740...$12.99

MOTOWN HITS
00311295...$12.95

PIAZZOLLA TANGOS
00306870...$14.99

POP STANDARDS FOR EASY CLASSICAL PIANO
00233739...$12.99

QUEEN FOR CLASSICAL PIANO
00156645...$14.99

RICHARD RODGERS CLASSICS
00310755...$12.95

SHOUT TO THE LORD!
00310699...$12.95

SONGS FROM CHILDHOOD FOR EASY CLASSICAL PIANO
00233688...$12.99

THE SOUND OF MUSIC
00119403...$14.99

SYMPHONIC HYMNS FOR PIANO
00224738...$14.99

TREASURED HYMNS FOR CLASSICAL PIANO
00312112...$14.99

THE TWELVE KEYS OF CHRISTMAS
00144926...$12.99

WORSHIP WITH A TOUCH OF JAZZ
00294036...$12.99

YULETIDE JAZZ
00311911...$17.99

EASY PIANO

AFRICAN-AMERICAN SPIRITUALS
00310610...$10.99

CATCHY SONGS FOR PIANO
00218387...$12.99

CELTIC DREAMS
00310973...$10.95

CHRISTMAS CAROLS FOR EASY CLASSICAL PIANO
00233686...$12.99

CHRISTMAS POPS
00311126...$14.99

CLASSIC POP/ROCK HITS
00311548...$12.95

A CLASSICAL CHRISTMAS
00310769...$10.95

CLASSICAL MOVIE THEMES
00310975...$10.99

CONTEMPORARY WORSHIP FAVORITES
00311805...$14.99

DISNEY SONGS FOR EASY CLASSICAL PIANO
00144352...$12.99

EARLY ROCK 'N' ROLL
00311093...$10.99

EASY WORSHIP MEDLEYS
00311997...$12.99

FOLKSONGS FOR EASY CLASSICAL PIANO
00160297...$12.99

GEORGE GERSHWIN CLASSICS
00110374...$12.99

GOSPEL TREASURES
00310805...$12.99

THE VINCE GUARALDI COLLECTION
00306821...$14.99

HYMNS FOR EASY CLASSICAL PIANO
00160294...$12.99

IMMORTAL HYMNS
00310798...$10.95

JAZZ STANDARDS
00311294...$12.99

LOVE SONGS
00310744...$10.95

RAGTIME CLASSICS
00311293...$10.95

SONGS OF INSPIRATION
00103258...$12.99

SWEET LAND OF LIBERTY
00310840...$10.99

TIMELESS PRAISE
00310712...$12.95

10,000 REASONS
00126450...$14.99

TV THEMES
00311086...$12.99

21 GREAT CLASSICS
00310717...$12.99

WEEKLY WORSHIP
00145342...$16.99

BIG-NOTE PIANO

CHILDREN'S FAVORITE MOVIE SONGS
00310838...$12.99

CHRISTMAS MUSIC
00311247...$10.95

CONTEMPORARY HITS
00310907...$12.99

HOW GREAT IS OUR GOD
00311402...$12.95

INTERNATIONAL FOLKSONGS
00311830...$12.99

JOY TO THE WORLD
00310888...$10.95

THE NUTCRACKER
00310908...$10.99

BEGINNING PIANO SOLOS

AWESOME GOD
00311202...$12.99

CHRISTIAN CHILDREN'S FAVORITES
00310837...$12.99

CHRISTMAS FAVORITES
00311246...$10.95

CHRISTMAS TRADITIONS
00311117...$10.99

EASY HYMNS
00311250...$12.99

EVERLASTING GOD
00102710...$10.99

KIDS' FAVORITES
00310822...$12.99

PIANO DUET

CLASSICAL THEME DUETS
00311350...$10.99

HYMN DUETS
00311544...$12.99

PRAISE & WORSHIP DUETS
00311203...$11.95

STAR WARS
00119405...$14.99

HAL•LEONARD®

Visit **www.halleonard.com**
for a complete series listing.

*Prices, contents, and availability
subject to change without notice.*

0917